COPYRIG

MW01601567

God
Says I Have A Purpose

Hey, hey Genesis Gems!

"A Religious Storybook for children"

Copyright 2023 by Shamoya Barzey

Contact: guidedbygenesisbooks@gmail.com

Written by: Shamoya Barzey

Dedicated to all my loved ones, especially my beautiful and talented daughter, Sedaiya.

You can do all things through Christ!
(Philippians 4:13)

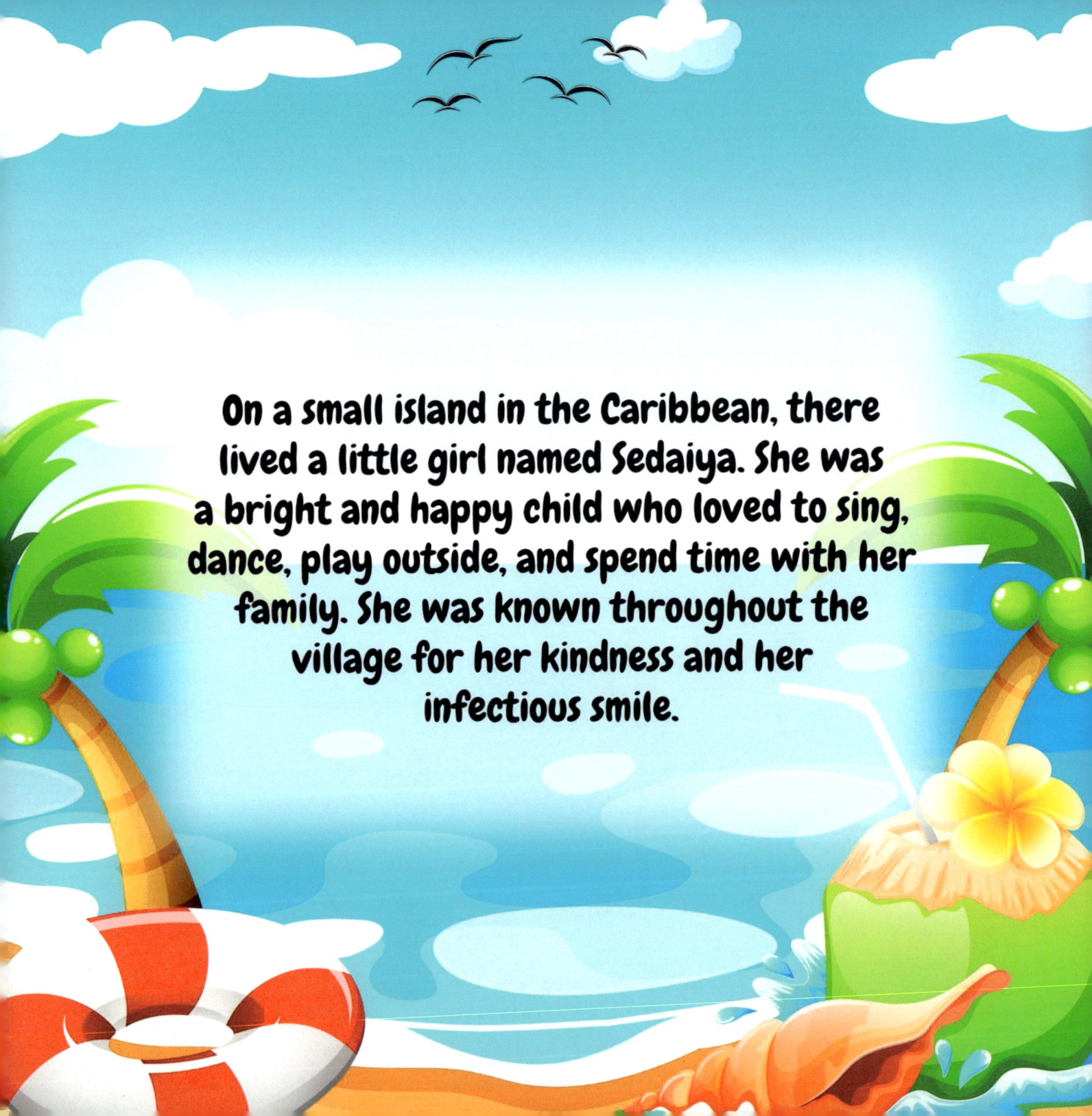

On a small island in the Caribbean, there lived a little girl named Sedaiya. She was a bright and happy child who loved to sing, dance, play outside, and spend time with her family. She was known throughout the village for her kindness and her infectious smile.

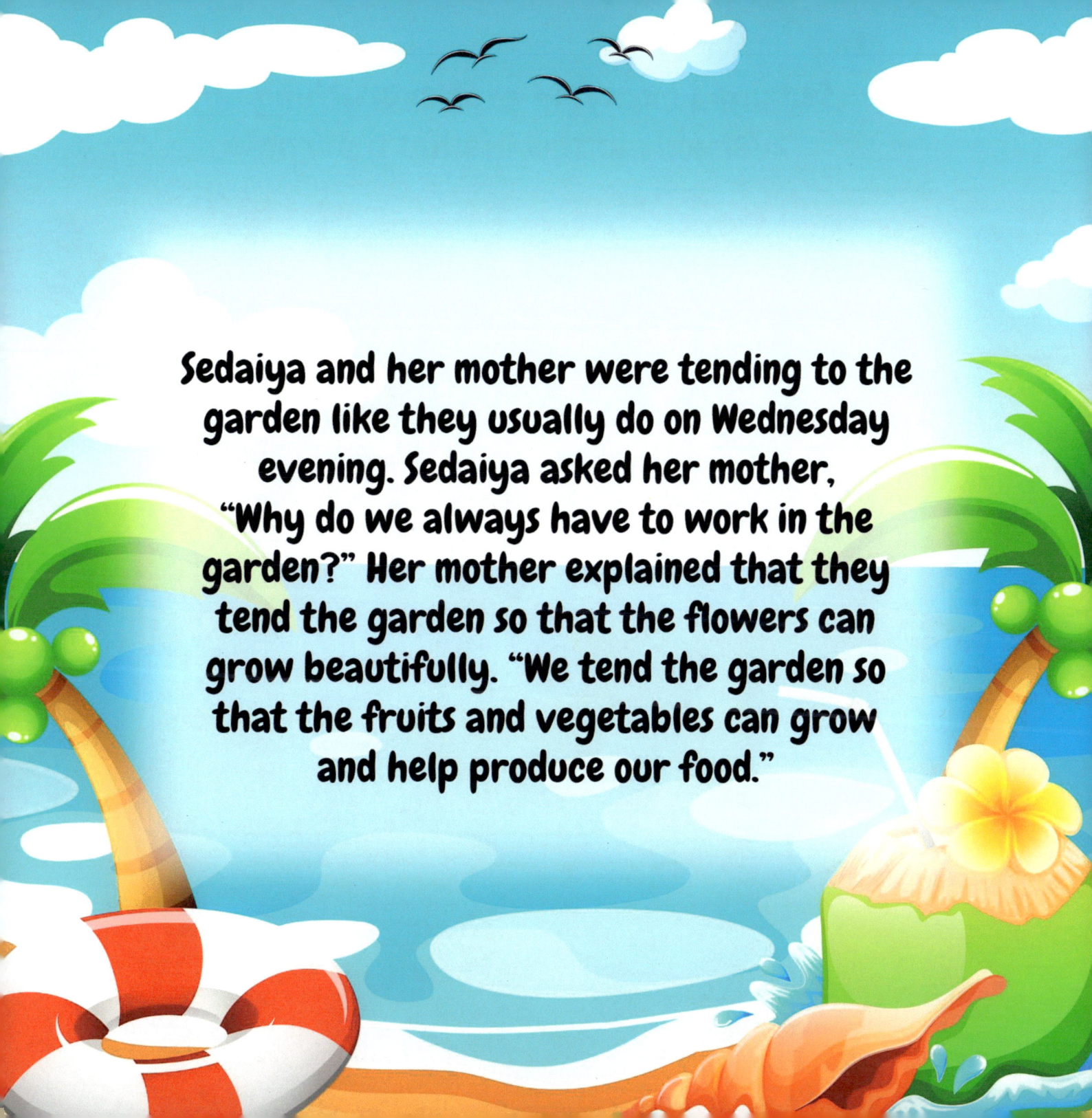

Sedaiya and her mother were tending to the garden like they usually do on Wednesday evening. Sedaiya asked her mother, "Why do we always have to work in the garden?" Her mother explained that they tend the garden so that the flowers can grow beautifully. "We tend the garden so that the fruits and vegetables can grow and help produce our food."

From the smallest insect to the largest object on this earth, God created them all with a purpose. If we did not tend the garden, we would have to go to the store to buy tomato paste to make tomato sauce for our pasta, instead of using the tomatoes from the garden.

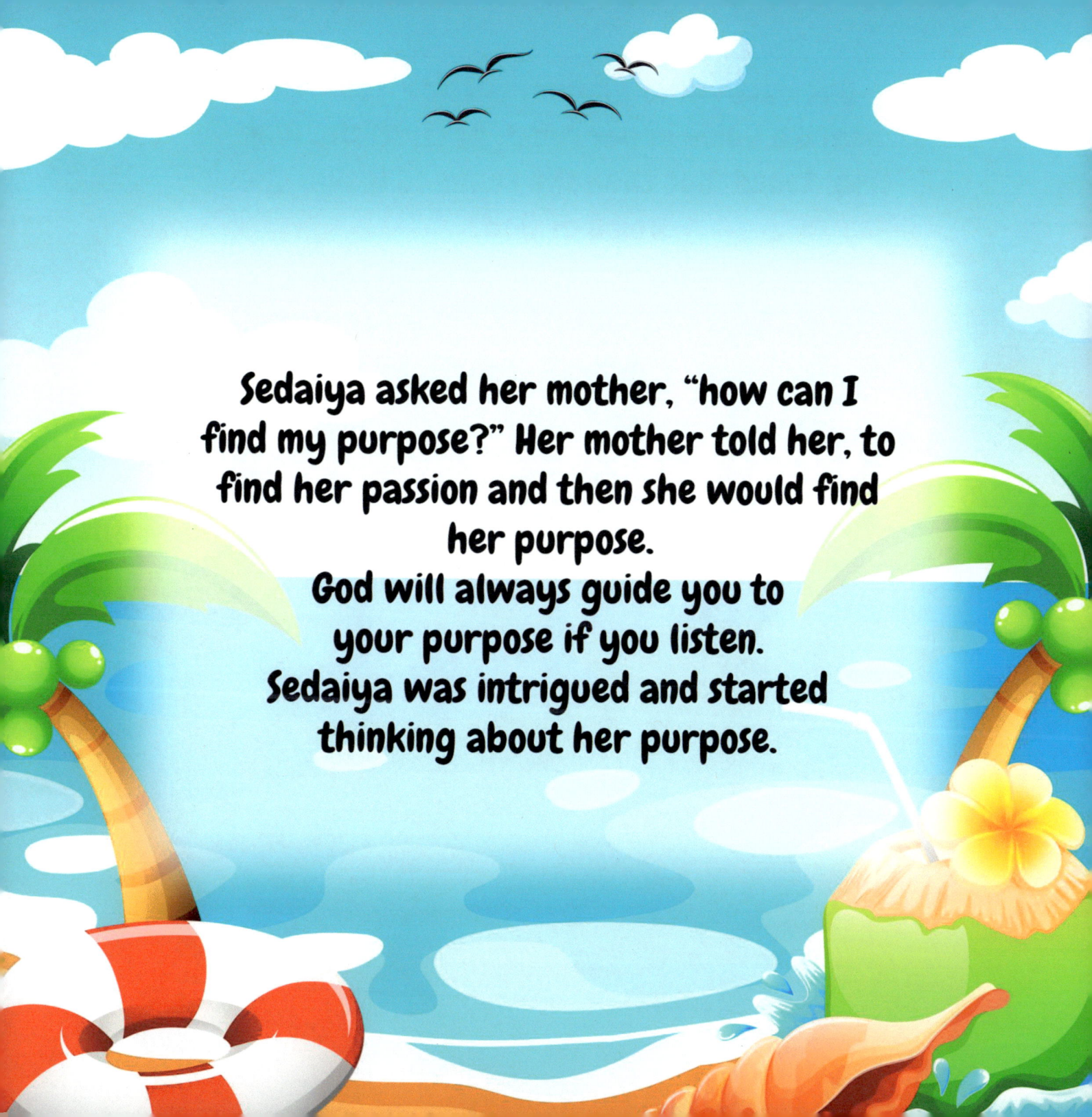

Sedaiya asked her mother, "how can I find my purpose?" Her mother told her, to find her passion and then she would find her purpose.
God will always guide you to your purpose if you listen.
Sedaiya was intrigued and started thinking about her purpose.

One day, while playing outside, Sedaiya heard a voice in her head. At first, she was frightened, but then she realized it was the voice of God.

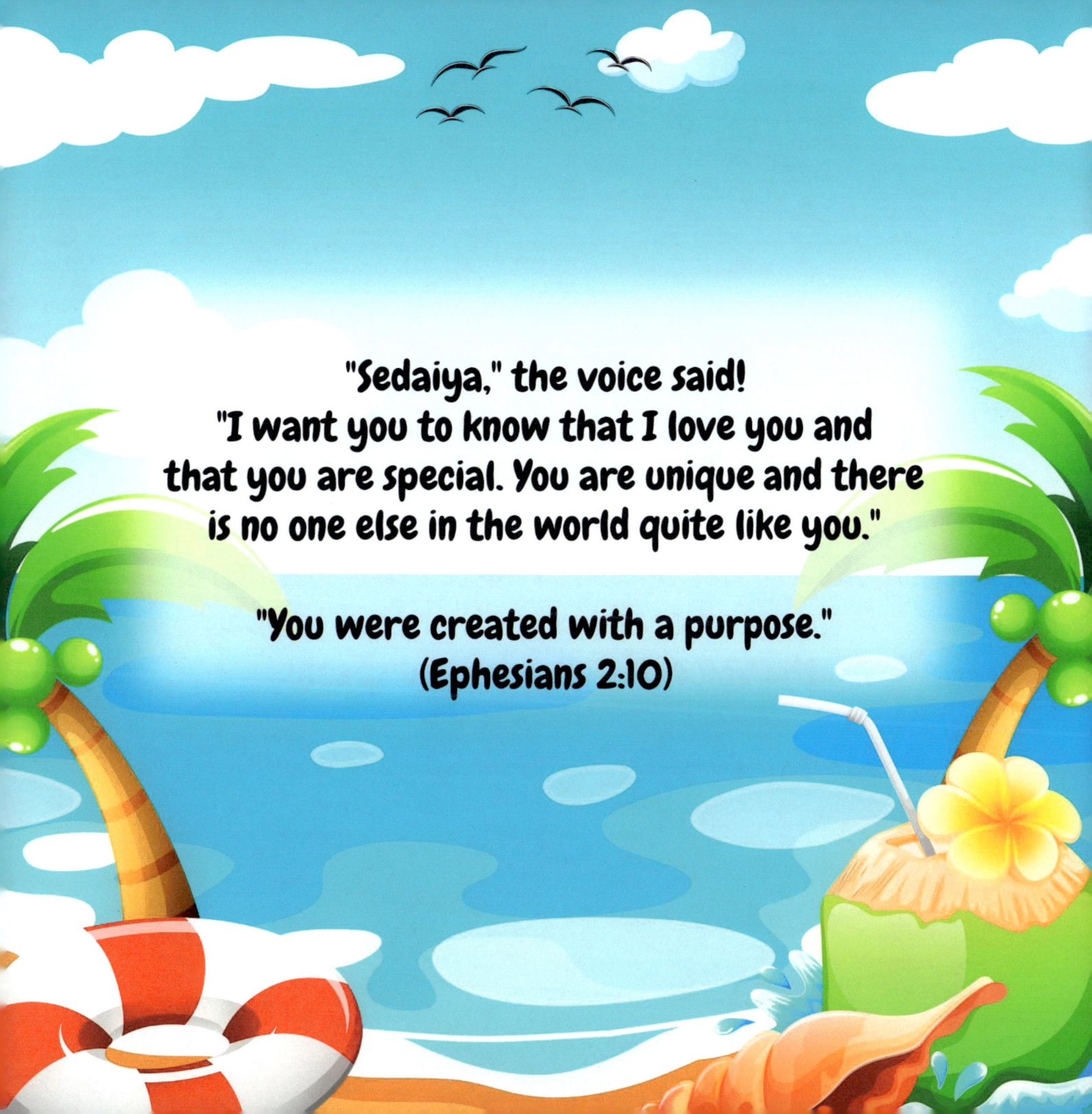

"Sedaiya," the voice said!
"I want you to know that I love you and
that you are special. You are unique and there
is no one else in the world quite like you."

"You were created with a purpose."
(Ephesians 2:10)

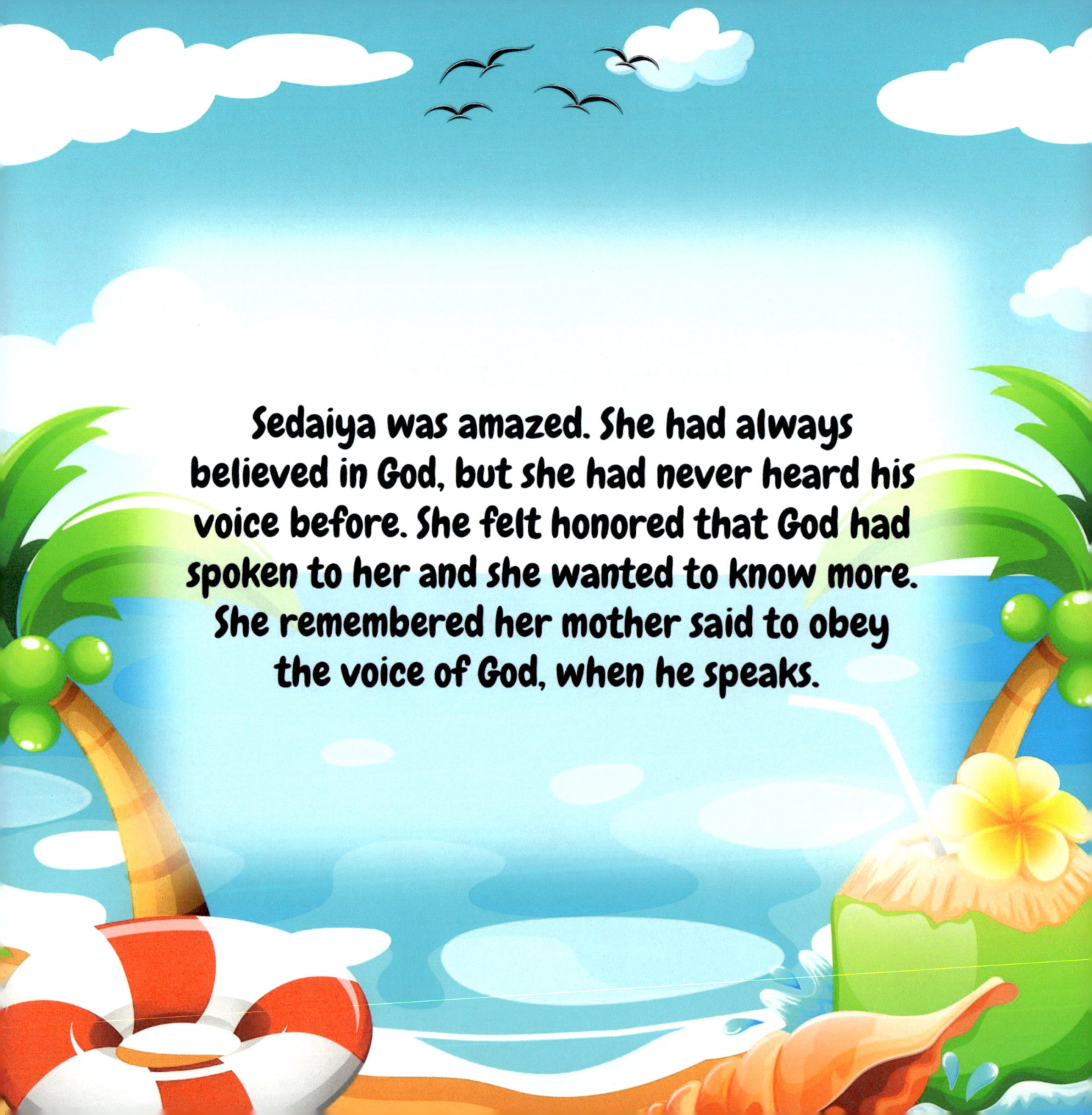

Sedaiya was amazed. She had always believed in God, but she had never heard his voice before. She felt honored that God had spoken to her and she wanted to know more. She remembered her mother said to obey the voice of God, when he speaks.

"God, how do you know that I am special," Sedaiya asked?

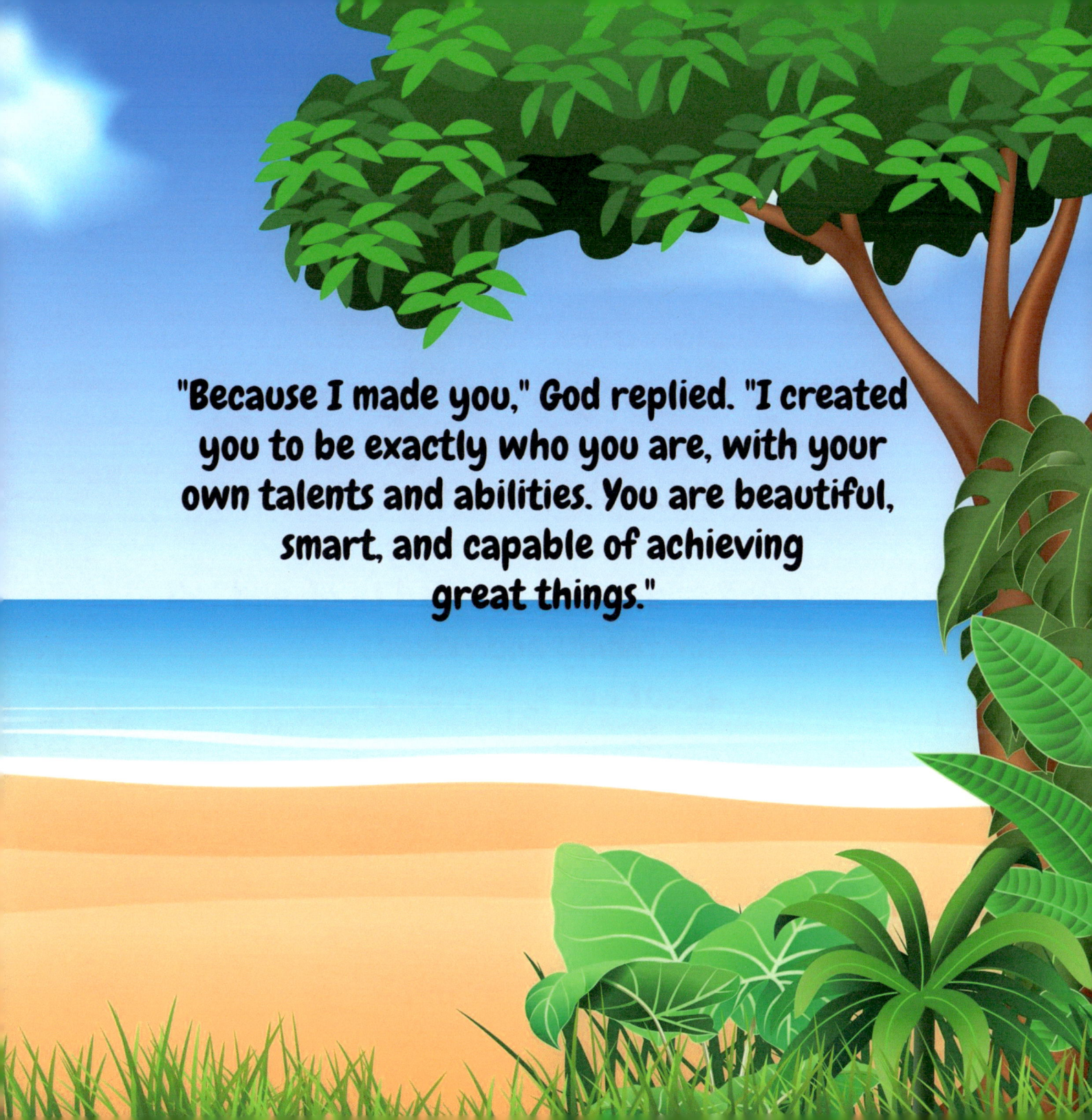

"Because I made you," God replied. "I created you to be exactly who you are, with your own talents and abilities. You are beautiful, smart, and capable of achieving great things."

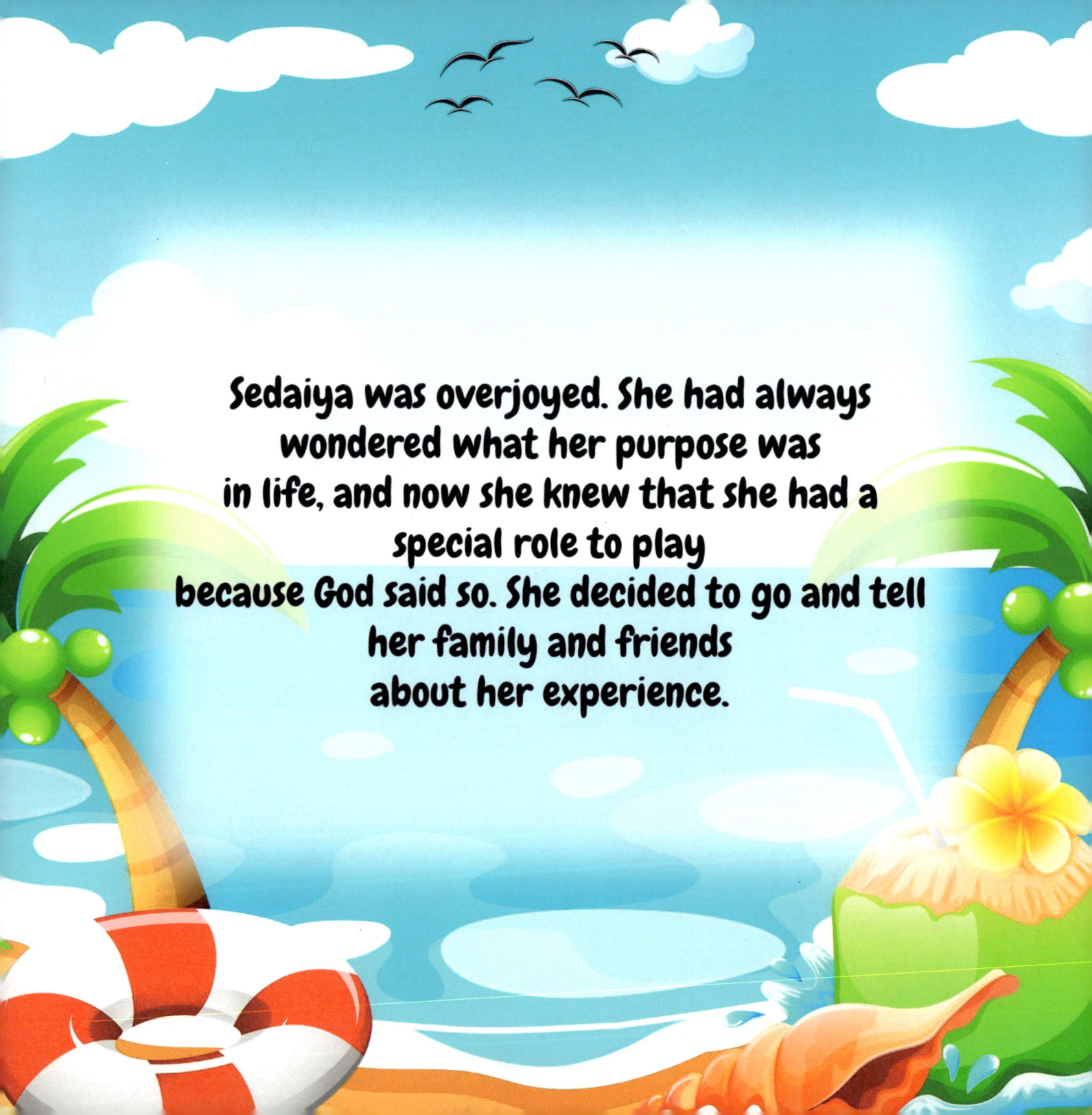

Sedaiya was overjoyed. She had always
wondered what her purpose was
in life, and now she knew that she had a
special role to play
because God said so. She decided to go and tell
her family and friends
about her experience.

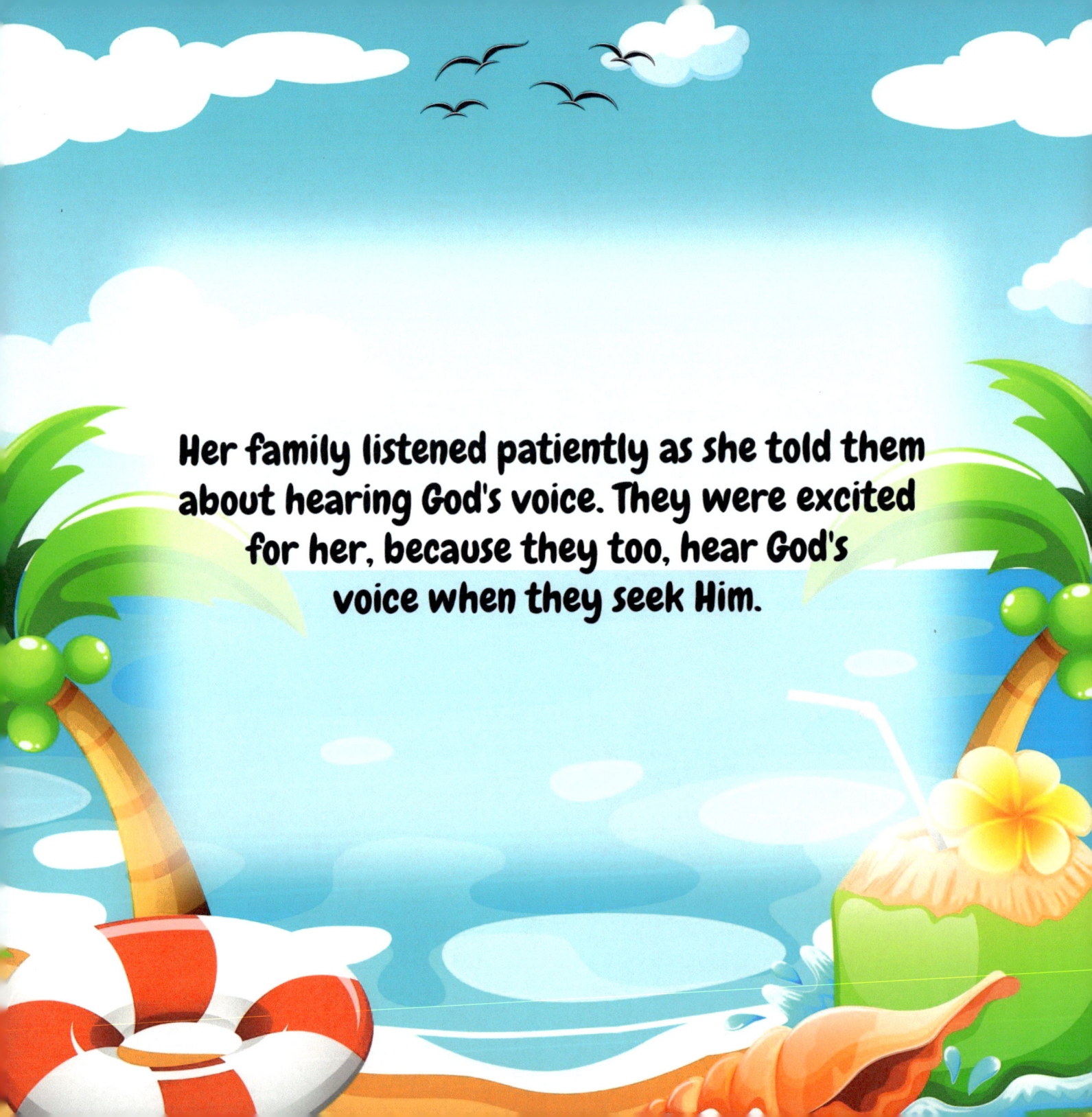

Her family listened patiently as she told them about hearing God's voice. They were excited for her, because they too, hear God's voice when they seek Him.

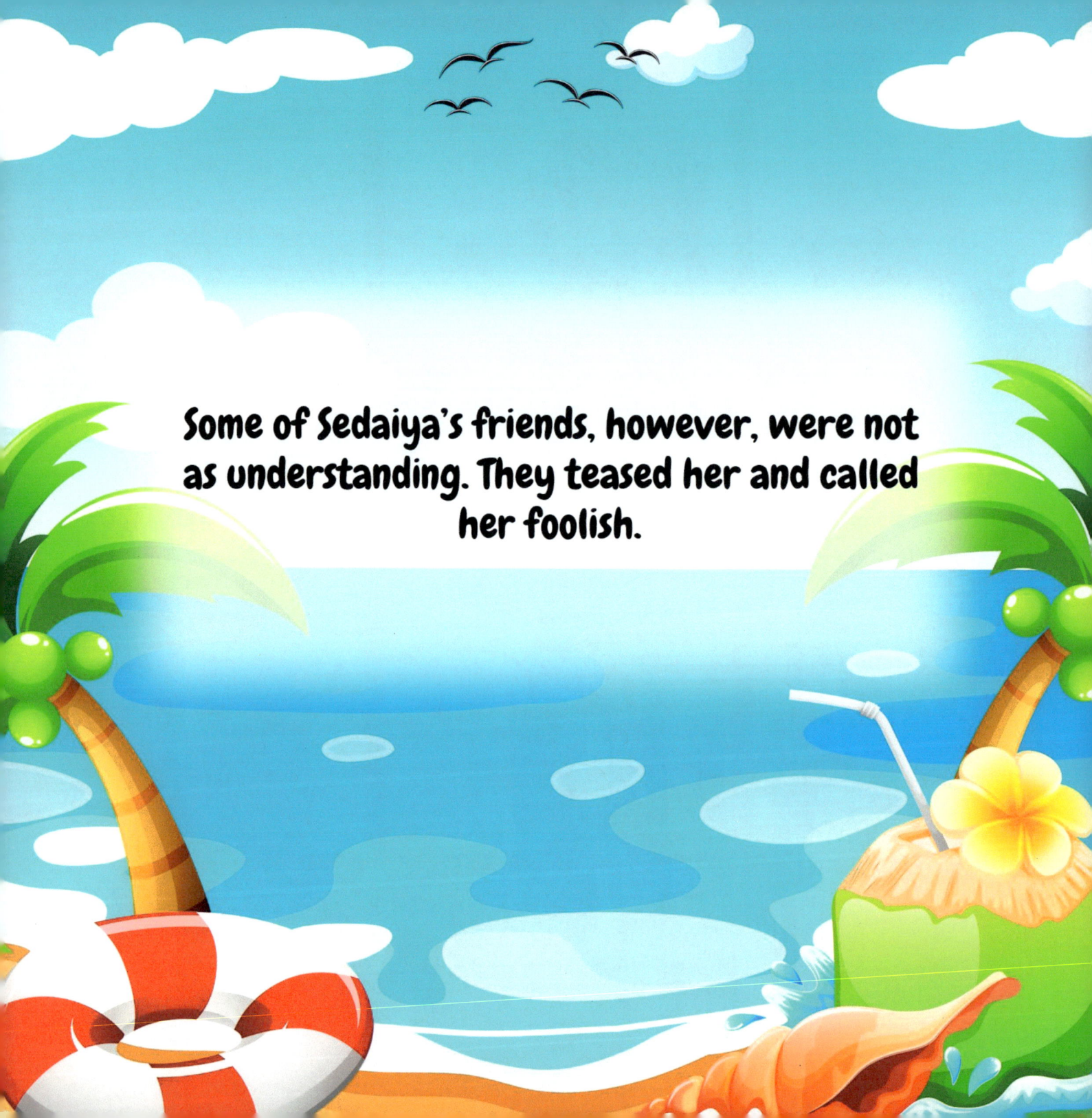

Some of Sedaiya's friends, however, were not as understanding. They teased her and called her foolish.

Sedaiya was hurt by their reaction, but she knew that what she had experienced was real. She decided to pray to God and ask for his guidance.

"God," she said, "I am thankful that you spoke to me and told me that I am special. But my friends don't believe me, and I don't want to feel alone. What should I do?"

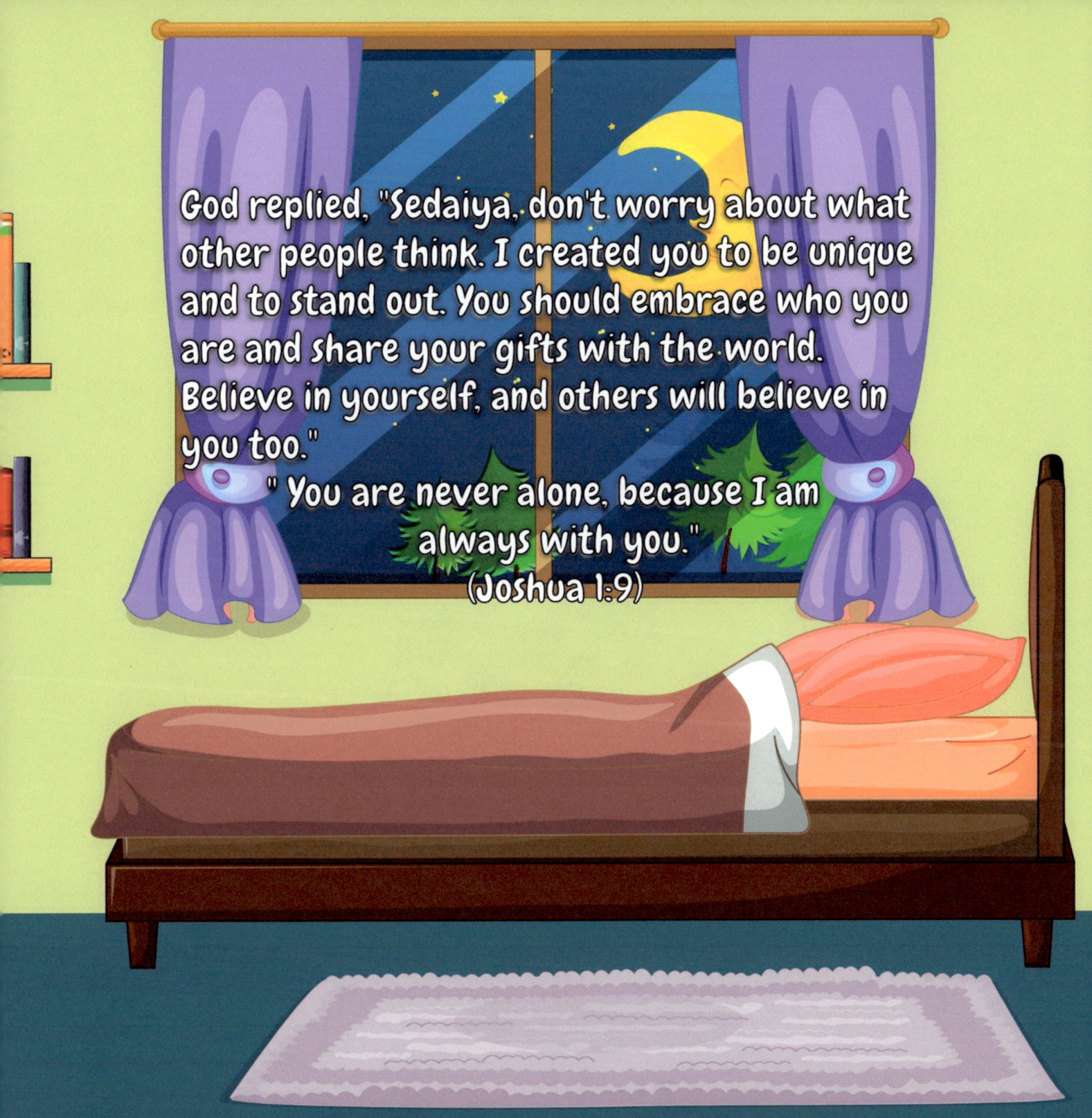

God replied, "Sedaiya, don't worry about what other people think. I created you to be unique and to stand out. You should embrace who you are and share your gifts with the world. Believe in yourself, and others will believe in you too."

" You are never alone, because I am always with you."
(Joshua 1:9)

Sedaiya took God's words to heart. She continued to pray and to listen to God's voice for guidance.

She discovered that she had a talent for writing songs and decided to start a Songwriters Club at school. She wrote a song for her school's talent show. She titled it, "God says I am."

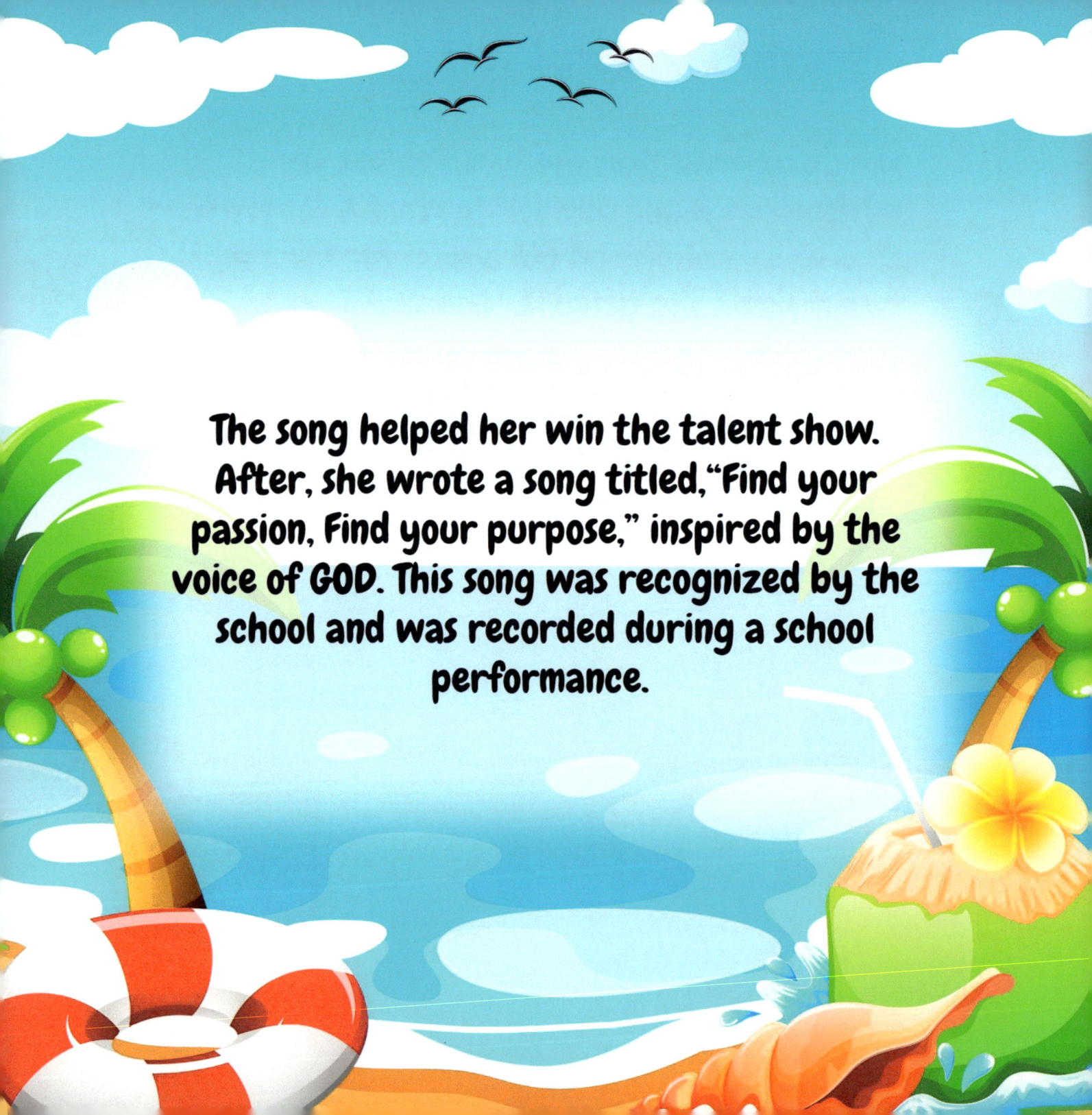

The song helped her win the talent show. After, she wrote a song titled,"Find your passion, Find your purpose," inspired by the voice of GOD. This song was recognized by the school and was recorded during a school performance.

Before Sedaiya knew it, she was trending on Youtube, Instagram, TikTok and other social media platforms. People from all over the world were inspired by Sedaiya and the words within her songs. They realized they too were special and that God had created them for a purpose. Sedaiya's friends also listened to and loved her songs. They realized that they had been wrong to doubt her.

From that day forward, Sedaiya realized her purpose was to help others find their purpose through her music. She continued to listen to God's voice and to embrace who God created her to be.

She knew that she was loved by God and that she was capable of achieving anything she set her mind to. Whenever she felt uncertain or alone, she would remember God's words, "You are special, and I love you. I am always with you."

The End

Ecclesiastes 3:1-
There is a time for everything, and
a season for every activity
under the heavens.

Jeremiah 29:11-
For I know the plans I have
for you, declares the LORD, plans to
prosper you and not to harm you, plans
to give you hope and a future.

Job 42:2-
I know that you can do all things;
no purpose of yours can be
thwarted.

Deuteronomy 5:33-
Walk in obedience to all that the Lord you
God has commanded you, so that you may live
and prosper and prolong your days in
the land that you will possess.

Made in the USA
Columbia, SC
06 February 2026

78874091R00020